YOUR SECRET OPERATOR
The Answer To Your Prosperity
Sonya Hylton

© September 2019 by Sonia Hylton

All rights reserved worldwide. This book is protected by the copyright laws of the United States of America.

No part of this publication may be reproduced, distributed, or transmitted in any form or by any means, including photocopying, recording, or other electronic or mechanical methods, without the prior written permission of the publisher, except in the case of brief quotations embodied in critical reviews and certain other noncommercial uses permitted by copyright law. For permission requests, write to the publisher, addressed "Attention: Permissions Coordinator," at the address below.

Published by Pecan Tree Publishing
September 2019
Hollywood, FL
www.pecantreebooks.com
adminservices@pecantreebooks.com

978-1-7341058-0-3 Paperback
978-1-7341058-1-0 Digital
Library of Congress Control Number:2019915212

Cover and Interior Design by: Charlyn Samson

Pecan Tree Publishing
www.pecantreebooks.com

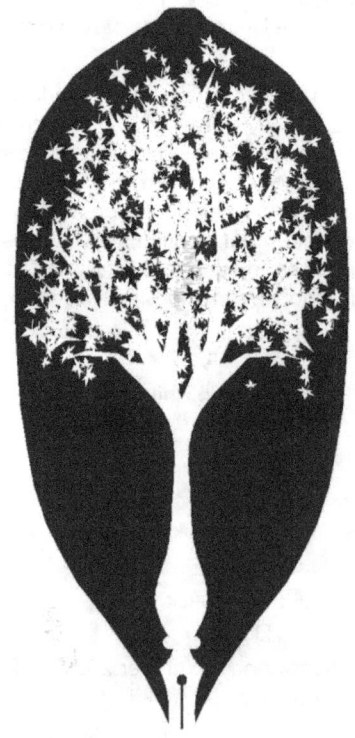

New Voices | New Styles | New Vision –
Creating a New Legacy of Dynamic Authors and Titles
Hollywood, FL

THOUGHTS ON YOUR SECRET OPERATOR

"Your Secret Operator" is a must read. It encourages you to take a look in the mirror at your own life in order to push through the walls of egotism and fear. Not only did I do some self-reflection but by doing so my level of spiritual consciousness was elevated. Transform your mind so you can transform your life. Again, a must read. Thank you for sharing your journey with me.

—Alice H. Everett, Entrepreneur

This book is a must-read for anyone making changes in their lives, especially for students like me. It's easy to follow with plenty of practical examples, and I've already begun to see results. The insights I gained from this book will definitely last a lifetime.

—Christopher Hylton, Student

They say that the mind is a terrible thing to waste. That's why "Your Secret Operator" is so valuable; it helps to train the mind into thinking into results. This book is simply AWESOME!

—Joel Gresham, Artist. Author

"Your Secret Operator" is a mind boggling yet inspirational must read. The various principles are an introduction for further exploration. This journey will definitely lead to something special.

—Maltimore Reynolds,
CEO Imperial Group Inc.

DEDICATIONS

This book is dedicated to my three sons, Dayon, Richard and Christopher. Through the years you have been caring, considerate, supportive and most of all independent.

Thank you, those qualities meant so much to me during the past years and during the writing of this book.

ACKNOWLEDGEMENTS

I am of the belief that anyone who has achieved anything of great consequence did not do it alone............they had a group of people who were firmly behind them, not only doing the daily tasks, but were also encouraging and supportive. Some of these people may not know the part they played in your success.

With that being said I acknowledge the following persons who were a part of my journey.

To David Imonitie, a former member of the Net Work Marketing Company, Organo Gold I say thank you for producing that CD Conceive, Believe and Achieve. Although we do not know each other personally your CD opened my eyes to the fact that extraordinarily successful people knew something that many do not know; that success secrets are documented in books. In your CD you mentioned persons that I had no familiarity with; Napoleon Hill, W. Clemente Stone and among many others, only one that I had some familiarity, Earle Nightingale.

Earle Nightingale's *The Strangest Secret* led me to what I can only describe as a 'reading frenzy". After a year of failing to accomplish the simple 30-day challenge and reading nearly 100 books I was like a person trying to find her way through a jungle of ideas, principles, etc. At the point of frustration in walked Bob Proctor with his coaching programs and seminars.

Bob you taught me to give gratitude everyday but most importantly you cleared a perfect path through my intellectual jungle and provided a strong foundation upon which I could build on the knowledge on how this Universe functions. You are everyday on the first line of my Gratitude Journal. I am so grateful that you came along.

Josette Killion (Josette KS), we have never personally met, but since 2016 we have daily met on Zoom or on the telephone for our hour of studying. You brought so much clarity to areas that were still cloudy, you introduced authors and teachers that I had never heard about. We both painstakingly and repeatedly went through the works of Thomas Troward, Neville Goddard, Abraham Hicks, Joseph Murphy among others until we got clarity. I could not have written this book without the insights you brought to our study hour; I than you.

To my Master Mind Team Josette, Eddie Cressy and Kathy Vogel, thank you for the support you gave on our weekly Master Mind calls. Again, we have never met but being graduates of Bob's Coaching Program you encouraged, pushed and spurred me on; for this I am forever grateful.

To my good friends Alice Everett, Maltimore Reynolds and Joel Gersham, thank you so much for your input and encouragement. Joel you gave me of your skills as an author and you provided clarity when there was confusion. I am forever grateful.

To my Publisher, E. Claudette Freeman and the Pecan Tree Publishing team (Kerry-Ann, Rodolfo, and Charlyn); thank you for your input and your patience.

This may seem strange, but I must acknowledge technology in the form of Amazon, YouTube and all the persons who posted videos. These entities have been invaluable in providing information with ease; they did the research for me.

Finally, to my three sons, Dayon, Richard, and Christopher; your support has been invaluable. Dayon you were always there shuffling me to and from the airport when I attended seminars and trainings. You took time off from work to chauffer me when I was unable to move around freely because of a leg injury, you were invaluable.

Richard, you know what it is to be patient. You coaxed and encouraged me through my social media and IT challenges. You helped to pull the potential that you saw in me out, even when I had difficulty seeing. To encourage me, you took a simple picture of me and created a mock book cover even before it came into my consciousness that I was going to write this book. When the title of the book came to me, months later, your mock cover provided the idea for the template. You definitely helped create my future. Christopher, thank you so much for your suggestions, and your linguistic skills; you so patiently did my first edits, and I am grateful.

CONTENTS

Acknowledgements...7
Introduction..15

Chapter 1: Life; Could This Be Your Experience?
           21
Chapter 2: Who Am I? 33
Chapter 3: Mind...43
Chapter 4: Man's Conscious and Subconscious
            Mind..47
Chapter 5: Thoughts: Our Tool 65
Chapter 6: What Do You Want? 77
Chapter 7: Alignment with the Idea...................91
Chapter 8: Affirmation, Autosuggestion and Self-
            Talk..103

Meet the Author..117

YOUR SECRET OPERATOR

THE ANSWER TO YOUR PROSPERITY

DR. SONYA HYLTON, PHARM.D.

INTRODUCTION

Years ago, during the transition from paper to digital, I was using a computer at my school to register for classes. I had no idea what to do. My ego prevented me from asking; I couldn't reveal that I didn't know how to register via the computer. It somehow appeared that everyone except me knew what to do. Much time passed while I was trying to figure it out, and my frustration was not helping. Then I noticed a sign next to the computer that read: "WHEN ALL ELSE FAILS, READ THE INSTRUCTIONS." I wasn't the only one who didn't read the instructions. Have you ever been in such a situation?

For many, life is like that; we ignore the instructions on how to live a fulfilling and prosperous life. When we finally read the signs, when we finally figure it out, "you will have one foot in the grave", as a friend of mine once said.

Some thought the instructions were outdated; they were for an ancient era, and now we are living in a modern world, so the instructions no longer apply. It's possible that the instructions, although simple, are not readily understood and some may have given up trying to understand them. Their simplicity didn't make any sense (, life is complicated), not realizing that ignoring the instructions would complicate life. Everyone in their mind must decide what a fulfilling and prosperous life is for themselves. Whatever it is to each person, the question then becomes: "if we should consider life an exam, would you give yourself a passing grade?"

It is said that 3% of the population controls 97% of the wealth. How do you feel about that statement? It is further said that if all the wealth in the world were collected and distributed evenly between everyone, in a short 10 years, it would flow right back into the hands of those who currently have it. That is, out of the hands of the 97% who currently don't have it and back into the hands of the 3% who do. You may think this is unfair, but the compelling question is: "why is this so?"

Money is an objective measure, and as such it's more readily and easily used for comparisons. But what about health, peace of mind, happiness, and wellbeing—states that cannot be numerically compared? The disparity does not only exist in our financial affairs, but in other areas of our personal, professional, and business lives to varying degrees. Could the disparity be due to a lack of understanding of who we are and the laws that govern our being?

As an individual, as in any discipline, industry, or in society, as knowledge increases, understanding improves and our lives change for the better.

Consider the source of the energy we use in our everyday lives to read and power our homes, vehicles, and business places. We started with the candle, kerosene, and coal that gave way to natural gas, electricity, and nuclear energy, and now we power our buildings with energy from the sun. This is the result of increased understanding and application of knowledge.

Medicine can now regularly replace diseased organs with those from another person; that could not be done hundreds of years ago. Skyscrapers didn't exist 500 years ago, but engineers have accomplished a feat where 1000 families can be housed using the same plot of land that formerly could house only 6 families. No longer do we have to send a letter via the Pony Express to communicate with someone 2,000 miles away; using some electronic device, we can not only instantly speak with them but also see them in real time. All these things happen because of research and the application of knowledge.

What about the instructions on how to live our lives, and on the reasons why our lives are the way they are? Do we still understand them as they were given to us as children or how they were given to us thousands of years ago? Or is there now further understanding that explains those instructions, knowledge that lets us understand what we are doing and why we do it? The original truths that brokered the instructions have not changed, neither can they be changed. However, our modern thinkers—philosophers and scientists—with a better understanding of the original truths can now tell us how to create the life we dared to dream of, and how to create a less complicated life.

Have you ever watched a magician perform his tricks? It's magic because you don't know how it is done; after you learn how, it is no longer magic. The same applies to our lives; good things and bad things happen as if by magic. Something unexpectedly happens to us or someone we know; if it's something positive we may call it good luck, and if it's something negative, then it's bad luck, implying that we or the person had absolutely nothing to do with what happened: it happened by chance.

The modern Self Development authors tell us that it's neither good luck, bad luck or a miracle that happens to us. Instead, it is just what happens, by the law of our being, when we allow certain thoughts to occupy our mind, and we have given our attention to them; that we absolutely had everything to do with what happens.

If one believes the philosophers and scientists, who among us wouldn't want to understand more? They have some of the answers to this phenomenon called life that we are trying to get a grip on before it permanently leaves us.

Humankind is forever evolving, which takes place through the attainment of knowledge. Knowledge dispels ignorance, another name for a lack of understanding. The human potential is unlimited; because knowledge is infinite, no individual or group is ever at a point of awareness that they understand everything. We are forever asking questions, and we receive answers. We not only consciously and unconsciously build on what those who lived before us have learnt; we also seek to clarify, to understand, to implement what we have learnt. What use is knowledge if it cannot be implemented in our everyday lives? At this point in the human experience there is enough information available to broaden the physical, mental, and spiritual aspects of our personality, such that anyone can make a significant change in his or her life experience. An understanding of the spiritual nature of ourselves is the "key to the kingdom."

There are truths that have been documented for thousands of years. By producing the same results time and time again, they will prove themselves to be the truths that they are. Socrates encourages us to: "Employ your time in improving yourself by other people's writings, so you shall come easily by what others have labored hard for." And Solomon says: "Do yourself a favor, love wisdom; study and watch your life grow and prosper."

Without the knowledge of who we are and the laws that govern our being, life will always be a mystery. We are already living life; we just have to understand how it works to make it better, if that is the desire. Today's technology gives us such easy access; our gaining understanding is only a "click away." We all have the potential and the power to be, to do, and to have any desire that we can imagine and believe in. However, you must first understand "Your Secret Operator".

CHAPTER 1

LIFE; COULD THIS BE YOUR EXPERIENCE?

"Life is a lottery that we've already won. But most people have not cashed in their tickets."

—*Louise Hay*

Right now, if you ask people on the street about the life they are experiencing, some of the answers would be: "Life is a struggle, life is hard, life is just not happening, life is OK," etc. The reality that is spoken is the same that the person has been speaking to themselves and others for a long time. We experience this every day during greetings, for example our co-workers: "How are you?" Most of the time, the response is the same and always fits the person's demeanor. It is their reality, so they tell it as it is. In telling it as it is, he or she is ignoring a simple instruction that has been given to us: "Let the weak man say: "I am *strong*" Would you consider the weak man saying he is strong a lie? The weak man wants to be strong, that is his desire, the answer to his problem of being weak. This quote may be recognized as coming from the scriptures. Most of us believe or want to believe what we have heard or read regarding the scriptures. However, if this knowledge were not applied (that is, if the instructions were not followed), how would we know what would happen when the weak man says: "I am strong"? Based on this profound eight word piece of instruction from our scriptures, the answer to the questions asked above should then be: "I am having a great life, I am having an easy life, I am having great things happen in my life," etc. Just as the weak man wants to be strong and was instructed to claim that strength, we must know what type of life we want and claim it. Those were the instructions given. Nat King Cole in his song *Pretend* also told us to: "Pretend you are happy when you are blue........."

James Allen in the early 1900s wrote these words in his essay *As A Man Thinketh:* "Humanity surges with uncontrolled passions, is tumultuous with ungoverned grief, is blown about by anxiety and doubt.........." We are now fast approaching the end of the second decade of the twenty-first century, and although it has been over one hundred years, the individual experiences of the greater part of humanity remain as what James Allen observed. There are some who believe that only about five percent of people are living the "good" life—good health, wealth, happiness, success, security, and a sense of wellbeing. During this same period, we have been given access to more knowledge than at any time in our history, and the information is becoming so much more accessible. Lives have improved, there is no doubt, but James Allen's statement still is true. This is happening because there is a part of our nature that remains a secret to us. We do not know that it is there, that we are interacting with it every moment, and that it dictates what we do. The life we live is dependent on what we do.

As humanity journeys through time, certain disciplines such as science, technology and medicine have advanced at such a rapid pace that textbooks are outdated before they are even printed. At the same time, in some parts of industrialized nations, it's as if time stood still; the lives of some people have not kept pace with advancing technology, science or medicine. Our knowledge allows us to diagnose and treat more illnesses than before, but at the same time there are more types of illnesses to treat.

An increasing number of individuals who never had a formal education are becoming more prosperous while an increasing number are graduating from colleges and universities and cannot find a job; society is wondering why, and rightly so. The old formula of going to school, getting a good education, and working for a good company with a good retirement plan and health benefits that will take care of the employee until he or she dies, worked for a while. Now, that formula is fast becoming obsolete.

There is nothing wrong with education, as it is the ticket to "freedom", and everyone should ensure that he or she receives one. Considering the changing global economic dynamics, what type of education a person can receive, and can it adequately supply the knowledge needed to sustain a lifetime of a good life? Napoleon Hill, in his classic *Think and Grow Rich*, says it pays to know where to buy knowledge.

How many companies, especially in today's economic climate, can live up to the obligations of the obsolete idea over the long haul? Companies go into business to make a profit, and so they will always try to maximize their profits. This sometimes means that they will automate for efficiency or take their production to another country where labor allows them to maximize the profits. The standard of living of these new employees will rise relative to their previous experience; but what about the previous employees? They are now without jobs.

When jobs are transferred in this manner, they are moving from a developed country to a lesser-developed country. We see a similar scenario plays out in families all the time, especially at the end of the year. People give away what they no longer need. What do they often do afterwards? They go out and get bigger and or better replacements. Nature does not like a vacuum; neither in our vegetable gardens, nor at the individual, local, national, or global levels. The space created will become occupied, sooner or later.

On the world stage where employees in industrialized countries lose their jobs to lesser-developed countries, how is this similar? When jobs leave, a vacuum has been created; the country and workers have the capability and the resources to reinvent themselves and fill the vacuum. With today's rapidly advancing technology such as self-driving cars, one can take the initiative to educate oneself. The advancing technology that robbed the workers of their jobs also provides the means for those same workers to create something bigger and better for themselves, oftentimes something that requires less time and less manual labor than their previous jobs.

This is not the first time that the world has experienced this change. In the Industrial Revolution when mechanization of the farms took place, those displaced workers went to the city to work in the industries (that had produced the equipment that took their jobs). The farms became more productive and efficient while an entire new workforce of factory workers and intellectuals (doctors, teachers, lawyers, grocery stores, beauticians, law enforcement agencies, hospitals, etc.) came out of the overcrowded cities with their new problems and abundant opportunities. These farm laborers had to relocate and re-engineer themselves; their lifestyle changed, oftentimes for the better. This time, with the technological age, the displaced workers do not necessarily have to relocate; the Internet is in homes and is rapidly becoming the new marketplace. Small businesses must start marketing themselves online and often do not know how. The world has suddenly gotten much smaller, as everyone is just a click away. Those who have chosen to jump in headfirst and learn this new economy are earning much more money in a fraction of the time than it would have taken them at the jobs they lost to automation and to other countries. In fact, for some, it is inconceivable that they could have earned so much at their former jobs.

Young people are drifting away from the economic situation of their parents. They still go to college, get professional degrees such as engineering and law, and sometimes start preparing for the new social media economy; they are learning to leverage technology and market products that they themselves or others have created.

Now the opportunity is there, just as it was during the Industrial Revolution, and a dog is never too old to learn new tricks. The world is always progressing; it cannot go backwards, and it cannot stand still.

The solution to a problem is always found in the problem. Technology was the problem for some, and technology has become and can become the solution for the same people. When travel agents lost their businesses to the Internet, some business owners started concentrating on tour groups, something the Internet travel space did not readily accommodate. Now, more people are travelling in tour groups than ever before; these business owners used what took away their income to secure even more income.

Price Pritchett in his book *The Employee Handbook of New Work Habits For A World Of Exponential Change* says this about the future: "We're entering a new era that requires us to reinvent not just ourselves and our organizations but also entire product categories and markets." The handbook makes reference to a study by McKinsey Global Institute that predicts that by 2030, worldwide, as many as 800 million jobs could be lost to automation, and the countries that will be most affected are the more advanced countries such as the U.S. and Germany. He points out that because technological change is exponential, in the 21st century we will experience not 100 years of progress, but what would be equivalent to 20,000 years (at today's rate). Ground Rule #6 of his 13 Ground Rules for Job Success is to "Stay In School." Prepare to fill the vacuum. He recommends adding more value to the workplace. "Make sure you contribute more value than you cost. Employees often mislead themselves, assuming they should get to keep their jobs if they're responsible and do good work. Some of them even have the idea that sticking around for a long time makes them worth more to the organization. Sure, experience may count for something. But maybe not. It depends on whether that experience really makes you worth more to your employer today, or whether it has mainly lost all value because the world is changing so rapidly."

Eric Hoffer during the last century predicted our changing world in these words: "In times of change, learners will inherit the earth, while the learned will find themselves beautifully equipped to deal with a world that no longer exists." Regardless of what we may believe, life is about continuous growth and learning, and whoever chooses to go against the natural tendency of the life process is going to be beaten up and run over by life itself.

How will these changes affect you and your family? In addition, what lifestyles are you experiencing right now; how is your health, both physical and mental, your relationships, your finances? Is your life balanced, is it what you expected it to be at this time of your life, or weren't there any expectations?

You may be one of many persons experiencing life at a place where he or she does not want to be. How long have you been trying to change things, or hoping and wishing for a change, but everything has remained the same? How long have you been stuck, trying to have a positive net worth, experience better health, better social interactions? Are you one of those people who feel the chills when you read Henry Clay's quote: "The time will come when winter will ask you what you were doing all summer?"

If you are not feeling ecstatic about the answers to these questions, part of the reason could be directly related to the knowledge you bought. Again, Napoleon Hill's quote: "it pays to know where to buy knowledge." A person may desperately want to change his or her situation; however, the thought of another certification, of going back to school, may not be appealing, especially if the current knowledge has not been producing expected results. There is another type of knowledge that is not taught in traditional institutions of learning; it has to be learnt in your free time; the initiative must be taken to seek it out and to learn it. No one really cares whether you learn it; there are no exams to be taken, no certificates to be had. However, you measure your own progress by the results you get in your life. It is often presented in seminars, webinars, online unofficial classes, do it yourself programs, and the like. Usually the people who attract this knowledge are those who have a burning desire for change; not a change that is casually discussed with friends, co-workers, relatives but a change that stems from a need coming from their 'core'. They sometimes would have started on a path where they are experiencing something different from the routine, and so the information finds them. A book, a seminar, a video may be mentioned by someone, a conversation that piques the interest.

This is the knowledge of knowing who we really are, the laws of our being that govern our lives, and understanding how to take control. This knowledge is unconsciously used every day; the challenge then is to learn what it is and therefore consciously use it to design our lives. Jim Rohn points out how these two different educational models can impact one's life: "Formal education makes you a living, self-education will make you a fortune." He also points out that: "Income seldom exceeds personal development"; he experienced both, going from milking cows to becoming a legend in the Personal Development Industry. Bob Proctor, another legend, maintains that one's income will increase as his or her level of awareness increases. He tells where at age 26, his life was a complete failure until a book on personal development, Napoleon Hill's *Think and Grow Rich*, was recommended to him. Back in the 1960s his annual income went from $4,000 to $165,000 in less than two years and to over $1,000,000 in about five years after he immersed himself in the philosophies that lead to success. All aspects of his life improved. You may not be impressed with money because you may have very little and don't know how to obtain more, or you may not have the need for any more than you already have; but the interesting thing is, this information impacts all areas of our lives, including our social life, business, family, relationships, and health.

We are now experiencing a world where many people are displaced in the job market; many will become entrepreneurs, their own bosses, while some will remain in the job market. They want to be successful in their new endeavors and many want to know how. The attitude to earning that a person has when he or she is being paid by someone else often cannot be the same when that person has to earn to pay him or herself. Whatever the endeavor may be, it is important to have an understanding that a person's future success has absolutely nothing to do with his or her past successes or failures; anyone can be successful.

I received an article from my neighbor: "300 Nurses Died By Suicide in Seven Years, Shows Alarming Stat", written by a Registered Nurse and was published in *Nurseslabs*, where there was a call for action on nurse suicides. The article in part reads "Figures released by the UK Office of National Statistics (ONS) last year showed that between 2011 and 2017 more than 300 nurses had taken their own lives, and that female nurses were

23% higher than the national average." A report published by the American Medical Association stated that in the age group 15-24, suicide was the 2nd leading cause of death, trailing behind deaths from unintentional motor vehicle accidents. Within this age group, in 2017 there was 47% more suicide among people aged 15-19 than in the year 2000.

James Allen's quote again comes to mind: "Humanity surges with uncontrolled passions, is tumultuous with ungoverned grief, is blown about by anxiety and doubt. "

Nearly all of a person's results in life is determined by how he or she relates to his or her 'Secret Operator', his or her subconscious mind. Moving forward in this rapidly changing world, there is a need for education outside of the traditional.

> *"Nothing in the world can take the place of persistence. Talent will not: nothing is more common than unsuccessful men with talent. Genius will not: unrewarded genius is almost a proverb. Education will not: the world is full of educated derelicts. Persistence and determination alone are omnipotent."*
>
> —*Calvin Coolidge*

CHAPTER 2

WHO AM I?

"Knowing yourself is the beginning of all wisdom"
—Aristotle

We look in the mirror every day and see a reflection of our physical self; we answer to a name that identifies us and we believe that is who we are. But, is this name who we are? Why does each of us need a name—why does anything need a name? One reason is to prevent confusion when we communicate with each other; to have the same points of reference, which leads to better understanding, clarity and ease.

Let us talk about Mate Vermon. When we talk about Mate, everyone in the conversation needs to know who Mate Vermon is. Mate Vermon lives on Blueberry Street; she works at Blueberry Hospital, has two children, is five feet eight inches tall, weighs about one hundred and forty pounds, and colors her hair pink and yellow. When Mate Vermon is the topic of conversation everyone has the same point of reference; there is no confusion. If Mate Vermon decides she doesn't like her name and changes it to Mary Brown, does that make her another person? No, it doesn't. So, what is it that makes her who she is regardless of the name she chooses?

One day John is walking down the street. He sees this young lady with pink and yellow hair and two kids, he automatically knows that she is Mate even after she had changed her name to Mary. So, your name identifies the person. That's all it does; it is not who you are.

John knew that the young woman was Mate because visual information gathered from his physical surroundings was relayed to his central nervous system. His brain interpreted the information presented to his conscious mind: yellow and pink hair, two kids, woman, Blueberry Street; conclusion.........Mate.

Mate Vermon a.k.a. Mary Brown is part of something much bigger than what John detected with his eyes, just as each of us is also a part of that bigger thing. There is a life force that is present everywhere; that is present in nature, is present in each of us. It is neither positive nor negative; it is energy, cannot be created or destroyed, and is always seeking to expand, to express itself more fully. Everything including each of us is a manifestation of this life force that we call Spirit.

In Mate as in each of us, a portion of this Spirit became physical to experience this world; it experiences it through us. Our physical body is the 'house' in which this Universal Spirit lives. That part of this Universal Spirit that is contained in each of us is who we are. Its inherent nature of life, love, beauty and a responsive, intelligent, creative force cannot be changed, regardless of the name we give to ourselves. It is the force that gives and maintains our life. Its creative nature is for our personal use, it communicates with us and we with it through feelings, we can think about it and communicate with it as we desire, and we can acknowledge its presence or choose not to.

Catherine Ponder in her book *The Dynamic Laws of Healing* says about us: "Man is about two percent physical and ninety-eight percent mental and spiritual." The teachings of Abraham documented in *Ask And It Is Given* by Ester and Jerry Hicks lead to the understanding that only a small part of a person's spirit is physically focused; the majority remains non-physical. This non-physical part is sometimes referred to as our Inner Being, the Source within each of us. Others choose to refer to this Universal Spirit as Divine Spirit, God, Jehovah, First Cause, Infinite Intelligence, Universal Intelligence, Divine Love, etc. Walt Whitman in the 1800s must have understood this concept of us that led to his statement "I am not all contained between my hat and my boots." What I see in the mirror is only a fraction of me, while Mate with her pink and yellow hair, five feet eight inches, and one-hundred-and-forty-pound frame is only about two percent of who she is.

We live in a universe where a power, a life force is always operating. We see it in the natural environment; the force guides the planets, the plant and animal life; that force is also in each of us. A force cannot be seen, but it can be discerned, so we know it is there. Since this is a force that we relate to, that we communicate with, it helps to have a visual representation of it.

Where the life force in us is concerned, it also helps to have an image that gives clarity to our structural relationship with it. A picture in our mind gives us something tangible to work with as we go about our daily lives. Each person can choose, if so desired, an analogy or image that works for him or her.

Using the hand as an analogy, as the image that creates order in my mind: Universal Spirit is the hand, and a finger is that part of the Spirit that is physically focused; that is the 'me' that others or myself cannot see. If the finger should be covered with a finger cot, that finger cot is what I see in the mirror, it is my body, the physical features by which others recognize me. When others get to interact with me, they get to know the spirit underneath the finger cot. When we get to know who we really are, we would have moved from seeing the finger cot, the physical body, to the awareness of our spirit that dwells within. Mary, as she now calls herself, is also Mate, the same person who lives inside the finger cot with the pink and yellow hair.

Each person represented by the finger is a finite being, but we are all a part of the entire hand that is Infinite, Universal. When the finger cot falls off, that is what we refer to as death; our spirit, our inner being continues to live forever. This inner being is perfection; it is forever a part of the Universal Spirit and so has to have the same characteristics. "Your spiritual DNA is perfect" states Bob Proctor; however, this perfection is not always evident.

Our inner being, our spirit, is a thinking substance. It expresses itself through us by way of our thoughts; its tendency is to guide us always to an expansion and fuller expression of itself, reflected in our personality. An expanded, more expressive life is reflected as joy, happiness, abundance, love, freedom, liberty, feeling good—not only for ourselves, but also for everyone else. It realizes that its Creator is the source of everything and cannot fail, so it also cannot fail. The Creator is all powerful, present everywhere, knows everything, and so does it. Comparatively speaking, the Creator is the ocean and each of us is a drop of water in that ocean. Whatever the characteristics of the ocean, is also the characteristics of the drop of water. The difference is in quantity and not in quality.

This information can be helpful to create the life we determine that we want to live. We all have access to the same Source; so why are we having such hugely different experiences? Some people live in multimillion-dollar mansions and some are living under the bridge; some support themselves and their family and some are dependent on others. Some are experiencing confidence and happiness, and some are experiencing doubt and worry. Some people are experiencing abundant health, and some are experiencing sickness.

The explanation for this difference is related to how the spirit operates and its relationship with us. Whatever the spirit contemplates itself to be, it becomes. Each of us is individualized spirit; therefore, whatever we contemplate ourselves to be, we become. With this knowledge, in evaluating what comes into our lives, we then become conscious that we cannot receive what we have not given our spirit to create.

We are pretty much like two persons in one: the YOU that is your Inner Being that has remained non-physical, and the you that is physical, that is guided by your individual subconscious mind, a. k. a. your Secret Operator. There is always a conversation going on in one's mind, between YOU and you; oftentimes there is a struggle. Sometimes we even have the discussion audibly; oftentimes that is when we are told:

"You are talking to yourself."

This 'Yourself' that you are talking to is the spiritual perfection that is your Inner Being. It is always a step or two ahead of you and it is always pulling you to expansion. When you act on its promptings you will find yourself in a better place. This is the gist of a conversation between YOU and you on a morning when there is a slight downpour of rain. Usually you would be up and into your two - mile jog before breakfast.

You: Oh well, it's raining. I think I'll skip jogging this morning.
YOU: It's not raining really hard; I think I should go.
You: It's a slight drizzle but where there is rain, there is the possibility of lightning.
YOU: I really should go.
You: There are leaves along the path; wet leaves are slippery. I'll go tomorrow; it's good to take a rest day.
YOU: I didn't go yesterday; I'll just go.
You: Tomorrow I'll jog four miles to make up for today.
You: (After some consideration) If I don't go, I'm just going to feel bad about not going, so I'll just go.

We have these conversations all the time with respect to all areas of our lives. When we end up doing what the bigger YOU is prompting us to do, we feel so much better about the situation and ourselves; the action leaves us in a better place. When the little you wins, we feel the opposite; the lack of action nags at us and leaves us at a worse place. It also robs us of our efficient use of time; we keep thinking about what could have been done. When we decide to do that which we are being called to do, knowing it is to move us forward, we feel so much better. It can be something as simple as the daily sorting of the mail.

When our thoughts and actions take us to a place where we are feeling really good, we can safely say we are in harmony with the bigger YOU. When we are not in harmony, we do not feel so good. Since YOU is our inner being which has remained non-physical and in direct communication with our Creator, our feelings then reflect how far we are removed from the 'thought pattern' of our Creator. The further we move away from this, that represents love, beauty and everything that is perfect, the worse we feel and the worse our situation gets.

Our Inner Being is about growth. At the same time, the little you that is controlled by the Secret Operator; our subconscious mind is always trying to protect us, to keep us comfortable. However, there is no growth in comfort and so we must continually override that inner talk from our subconscious mind that is intent on keeping us comfortable.

The Life Force cannot express variety through what exists in nature; it expresses variety through us, humans. Each person is endowed with six intellectual or mental faculties: perception, reason, intuition, memory, will and imagination, which allows us to communicate with our inner spiritual self. Most of us can also see, hear, smell, taste and touch; we have five physical senses that allow us to communicate with our outer environment. Our entire 'package' therefore consists of physical senses, mental faculties, a subconscious mind and an inner spiritual self that remains a part of Universal Mind; all rolled into one. We are self-contained; the power of the universe is within us; everything we have received and will receive comes from within us, from the spiritual aspect of us.

Humankind also received equal amounts of an extremely precious commodity: time. Everyone has twenty-four hours in each day; no one gets a second more or a second less. The different lives that we each live are directly related to how we use our 'package' in the twenty-four hours of each day. Our subconscious mind influences the decisions we make, the actions we take, and how we utilize each day. That in turn determines our results.

There is a part of ourselves that is perfect and is always striving for this perfection to shine through. The degree to which it comes through depends on the concept we have of ourselves, of our self-image. The concept that each person has of him or herself is dictated by the arrangement of the subconscious mind, and our mind is always arranged in the image of all we think, desire, love, believe is true and consent to; what we are conscious of. We are who we conceive ourselves to be, and so we can conceive ourselves to be whoever we want to be.

> *"You are a spiritual being, that's the essence of who you are. Spirit is all knowing, all-powerful, ever present; that's you. All the power of the universe is within you."*
>
> —Bob Proctor

CHAPTER 3

MIND

"The mind is a powerful force. It can enslave us or empower us. It can plunge us into the depths of misery or take us to the heights of ecstasy. Learn to use the power wisely."

—David Cuschieri

What is mind?

Oftentimes when we think of mind, we immediately think of our brain; however, our mind is not our brain. The brain is a product of the mind, it is the structure in our body through which the mind functions. Mind is Spirit. Mind is an activity; it is not a thing that is tangible, that you can see and hold. It is an activity that is present in every cell of the body. There is the Mind of the Creator, (Infinite Mind) and there is the mind of man. The mind of man is finite (analogy of the finger, a drop of water in the ocean) and the mind of God is infinite (analogy of the entire hand, the entire ocean). Each is a part of the other. God is the ultimate of forces, and so the Mind of God is the ultimate force. The mind of man is derived from the Mind of God.

Infinite Mind gave man two aspects of itself; the Conscious Mind and the Subconscious Mind. Man's conscious mind is that part of the Infinite Mind that has been given to us for our use so that we can function as individuals who make choices. The other part of Universal Consciousness that was given to man is an aspect of the Universal Subconscious Mind; this is man's subconscious mind. This is the part of man's mind that is always in contact with Universal Subjective Mind. This is the medium through which Divine Mind communicates with man. Working in conjunction with Universal Subconscious Mind, man's subconscious mind creates for him all the choices he makes with his conscious mind.

The Universal Subconscious Mind contains the essence of everything seen and unseen; this is energy that has the potential to become anything. The energy cannot express itself, as only humans can call it into expression; everything that man has in his life came from this source. Man has been given the power to call into expression anything that he can conceive of; all is in Universal Subjective Mind. *The Subconscious Speaks.*

Universal Subjective Mind is analogous to a gigantic warehouse and manufacturing plant, limitless and without boundaries that contains the "raw materials" for anything a man's conscious mind can conceive of. It not only holds the raw material; it produces the finished product. Each person decides what he or she wants and the universal forces acting through us put the necessary pieces together which then show up in our lives as things, situations and circumstances.

There is the belief that every person has a true destiny and that he or she is always in search of this state. This level of activity where this destiny originates is the Superconscious in each person, a place of perfection often referred to as Divine Mind or God. The Super Conscious activity is a deeper part of Universal Subconscious activity. When we converse with God this is the level of our mind activity. Florence Shovel Shinn refers to the Super Conscious mind as "The God Mind" within each man and is the realm of perfect ideas." Thomas Troward, in his essays *The Hidden Power* states: "The Supreme Mind with which we converse is only to be met in the profoundest depths of our own being, is more perfectly ourselves than our own hands and feet. It is our natural base."

We are always intrinsically connected to Divine Mind. The connection cannot be broken; it is there for our use. However, as Thomas Troward states, "It must be consciously realized before it can be consciously used." This aspect of Mind is perfection;

it guides us to all that is good, love, harmonious, perfect and abundant. We, because of our spiritual nature, sense this, so the question becomes: why are we not having perfect expression in all aspects of our lives? The answer lies in our individual subconscious mind, which I choose to refer to as 'Your Secret Operator.'

> *"There is one source from which all things come. The source is God. God is Spirit. God is mind. I am one with the Spirit and Mind of God."*
> —*The Subconscious Speaks*

CHAPTER 4

MAN'S CONSCIOUS AND SUBCONSCIOUS MIND

> *"Why is one person healed of a so-called incurable disease and another isn't? Why do so many good, kind religious people suffer the tortures of the damned in their mind and body? Why do so many immoral and irreligious people succeed and prosper and enjoy radiant health? Why is one person happily married and her sister very unhappy and frustrated? The answer to all these questions is found in the workings of the conscious and subconscious mind."*
>
> —Joseph Murphy

Man has one mind but two levels of activities, the conscious and the subconscious. Both activities are separate but intricately linked. A mental picture of an iceberg can be used to illustrate the relationship between the conscious and subconscious mind activities. The tip of the iceberg above the surface of the ocean is comparable to the amount of our conscious mind activity, about 5%, and the part below the surface of the water is the amount of our subconscious mind activity, 95%. It is like a secret within us; it operates very quietly, and its presence is not readily evident. Most people are not aware of its existence; however, it is responsible for our habitual behavior, and all our behavior is habitual. It dictates our daily actions and our actions determine our results in life. The part of our mind that few are conscious of, determines our life experiences.

Florence Scovel Shinn in her book: *The Game of Life and How to Play it*, refers to the conscious mind as the mortal or carnal mind. "It is the human mind and sees life as it appears to be. It sees death, disaster, sickness, poverty and limitation of every kind, and it impresses the subconscious." The scriptures refer to this conscious level of mind activity as the male that dominates the female, the subconscious mind. We are aware of our conscious mind because this level of activity connects us with our external environment via our five physical senses. Our six intellectual or mental faculties set us apart from all other forms of life that we are aware of. Our perception, reason, intuition, memory, will and imagination allow our conscious mind to create the life we want to experience. The conscious mind is personal, objective, rational, selective and is the thinking phase of mind. Its activity is in terms of time and space. It reasons inductively; that is, it gathers information, entertains different thoughts, makes comparisons of different facts, draws conclusions, and forms an idea. It reasons from observation, experience and education. It can access only a very small fraction of information that is available. As an analogy, if you are in your house and look at the outside through a keyhole in your door, you can only see what is within the outline of the keyhole. Should you open the door and step outside, you will see as far as your eyes can see. However, should you get in a spaceship and travel into outer space, not only will you see the earth, but other planets. Where access to information is concerned, the conscious mind can access only what can be seen through the keyhole. The individual's subconscious mind has immediate access to what is seen when the door is wide open; however, it also has access to what is visible from the spaceship and beyond. Our subconscious mind has access to all information.

All states of mind are within each of us and are linked to each other; our level of mental activity determines what level we access. Every thought that has ever been thought, every emotion that has ever been felt, every image that has ever been seen by every person that has ever lived, is present in Universal Mind. The individual's subconscious mind houses the individual's experiences, and the Universal Subconscious Mind, the experiences of all. The conscious mind can therefore get its information externally from the world around us, or internally by way of the subconscious mind: from the Divinity within us.

This information from Divine Mind comes to us intuitively. Some people jokingly refer to intuition as "God telephoning us," that feeling that makes you think of going somewhere right now; and when you get there, you meet someone whom for a long time you had wanted to see.

Recently I was coming home from an event. I got to the airport about four hours before my flight; I have never arrived at the airport that early before. As soon as I arrived, although I was not hungry, I decided that my companions and I would have something to eat to pass the time. As we were about to step onto the sidewalk towards the restaurant, I saw coming towards us a couple; friends of mine whom I had not seen or communicated with for years. They had been on my mind for quite a number of months, and now they were coming home from a visit to the United States. I had a desire to see them, and Universal Intelligence knew that they would have been at the airport at a certain time and therefore created a rendezvous. I was prompted to get to the airport unusually early and was again prompted to get something to eat although I was not hungry. Following these promptings placed me directly in the path of my friends. A few seconds before or after and I would have missed them. This scenario is usually referred to as chance or luck. If

I hadn't followed those promptings, I would have unknowingly missed them. If they were not on my mind a rendezvous would not have been created. We are often told to follow our intuition; the student in an exam understands what this means when he changes the first answer that came to his mind, only to find out that the original answer was correct.

About a year ago, my son had a deep desire to speak with a past high school acquaintance who had created a product that he was marketing in another country. The young man was a barber at the shop where my son sometimes gets his hair trimmed; he was due back home from his trip abroad. That Saturday about twenty minutes to closing time my son suddenly decided to get his hair trimmed. Although the shop was just across the street because it was close to closing time, he decided to drive instead of walk. I remember him coming back into the house three times after he initially left, and I thought the shop would be closed by the time he got there. When he returned home, he told me the most amazing thing happened; the young man he wanted to see was walking into the shop while he was going in. The young man had at the last moment decided to get his hair 'tapered,' which according to my son wasn't urgent because he always wore a baseball cap (the product he had created). If my son was not delayed three times, he would have missed the young man and left the shop because it was too late to get his hair trimmed. The universe is always collaborating with us based on the desires we have; that urgent thought to do a thing, to go somewhere is "God calling us on the telephone." We often think that we are orchestrating the actions we take; however, we are unconsciously responding to the promptings from our subconscious mind in response to the thoughts we have been thinking.

The conscious mind also reasons deductively. When we engage in activities that do not require much critical thinking such as listening to music or the radio, watching television, or painting, the information gets past our inductive reasoning mind through the deductive pathway into our subconscious mind. We are picking up information from these outside sources without critically evaluating them, and so they unconsciously pass into our subconscious mind. You may find yourself humming a song that you never consciously learnt; the lyrics got past your conscious mind without you being conscious of it; It went via the DEDUCTIVE pathway.

This is the major pathway through which children prior to the age of about six years old learn. Many parents have been embarrassed when their little ones talk about things in the presence of others that were meant for the family. Their inductive reasoning capability has not yet developed to the point where they can evaluate information received.

Our conscious mind, by inductive or deductive reasoning, chooses the life we want to experience, and the subconscious mind executes the plan. The idea chosen by the conscious mind is impressed on the subconscious mind in the form of the individual's feelings. In doing so, the individual is unknowingly accessing the contents of Universal Mind; the idea will be expressed in his or her life. The mechanism by which it gives form to ideas impressed upon it is unknown; however, whatever idea gets to this part of the mind has to be expressed.

The subconscious mind is very sensitive but is non-selective; it picks up our slightest doubts. It is impersonal; it doesn't consider if what is impressed on it is for the person's best interest or not, and the information that gets there is the initial cause of all of man's experiences.

Everything is already created and is in Universal Subjective Mind at different levels of vibration. Whatever man chooses to have for himself or others is at this level of mind activity. The various laws of the universe such as the Law of Attraction and other forces will attract to the person all that is required to fulfill the feeling that was impressed upon it.

The subconscious mind acts in the now; it has no concept of space or time; there is no past or future; everything is happening now. It is amenable to suggestions, both from the individual and those in his environment. An entire nation can be given suggestions; we see this happening during election campaigns. Some people, without any evaluation of their own, vote for whom they are told to vote for; they hate whom they are told to hate, and they love whom they are told to love. We emotionalize what we are hearing and seeing; those emotions are creative and will again be experienced in the future. The world has experienced wars because people en masse were given suggestions about others or about themselves. If the suggestion is heard often enough then the conscious mind will believe it to be true; the ideas will be impressed on the subconscious mind and the universal forces along with the laws acting on the spiritual part of our personality will lead us to actions to fulfill the idea. Adolf Hitler understood the power of the subconscious mind and its amicability to suggestion when he said: "How lucky for leaders that men don't think."

This is where we have our beliefs, the thoughts that we keep thinking. Our life is a mirror of the beliefs in our subconscious mind. James Allen spoke to this when he wrote: "A man thinks in secret, and it comes to pass; environment is but his looking glass." Nothing can be hidden; all ideas that are contemplated and emotionalized get to the subconscious mind and are expressed. However, no one knows when and the form in which they will be expressed.

Everything in the universe vibrates; our thoughts are at different vibrational frequencies and they give rise to our emotions. This emotional state determines the vibrational frequency of our subconscious mind. When this vibrational frequency matches the vibrational frequency of the selected contents of the Universal Subconscious Mind, the contents will be our experience. Vibrations that are associated with emotions such as fear, anxiety, hate, criticism and other negative emotional states result in sickness. Those associated with gratitude, kindness, happiness, love, beauty and other positive emotional states result in wellbeing. Whatever vibrational frequency we are transmitting, we will also receive. This principle is referred to as the Law of Cause and Effect or Sowing and Reaping. How we tune our radio illustrates this; should we tune our radio to 97.3FM, we will receive information that is transmitted on this frequency; we cannot receive information transmitted on the frequency of 105.1FM.

One of the most marvelous attributes of the subconscious mind that we can use to full advantage to get whatever we want, is that it does not know the difference between what is real and what is unreal. Its deductive nature doesn't allow it to question the information it receives; it just acts on it to its logical conclusion. Should it be told a lie, it will create whatever that idea embodies, and you will experience it. Some years ago, I had a deep desire to drive a Dodge 1500 Ram truck that was part of the business I was engaged in. While driving my regular car I pretended that I was driving a truck, actually much larger than the Dodge. At some point, it occurred to me that imagining, daydreaming is what children do, and I as an adult should know better. Soon after I ceased from the activity. Months later, there was an accident. The car was irreparable. That Dodge truck became my means of transport.

To the onlooker, I got the truck because I no longer had my car. However, that was a secondary cause; only I knew the primary cause. Of course, I did not realize this until years when I started studying. My subconscious mind got the suggestion of my desiring to drive the truck. I further gave it an emotional pattern of what I wanted; I was driving the truck in my imagination as if I already owned it. The subconscious mind, by the law of its nature, will always take to completion whatever emotion is imprinted on it. I imprinted the strong desire of wanting to drive the truck and I was behaving as if I had already received it. On closer examination you may realize that I was doing what the scriptures tell us to do when we pray, to believe that we already have the thing we are praying for, and we will receive it. In driving the truck in my imagination, I was fulfilling part of the requisites for an answered prayer. I unknowingly had been praying; the subconscious mind was given an emotion of my wish fulfilled. The only person who knew that I had a desire and pretended to drive the truck, was me. The first cause of everything is always in the spiritual realm of thoughts, never in the physical realm of things, circumstances and situations; these are secondary causes. The truck came into my life in a way that was easy and effortless. Andrew Carnegie summarizes this in the following: "Any idea that is held in the mind, that is emphasized, that is either feared or revered, will begin at once to clothe itself in the most convenient and appropriate form available."

The subconscious mind is the Life Principle that is present in us when we were born; it was there from the moment of conception and it never leaves us. The baby does not have conscious mind activity, only subconscious mind activity. It cannot sort information, cannot reject, cannot make decisions on what it is exposed to and so cannot prevent what gets into its subconscious mind. Everything that is being said, all the emotions, the ideas that are discussed, all that's in the baby's environment gets "downloaded" into its mind. If ideas of poverty and lack are the dominant ideas, the baby will grow up and these ideas will determine its thought patterns; if the ideas are wealth and abundance, these will determine the thought patterns. Until the child is about six years of age, when the conscious mind becomes fully functional, he or she is progressively at the mercy of the environment; school, home, relatives, community, place of worship, friends, shows on television, the games played, radio programs, visitors, etc. As the child grows into an adult, he will start entertaining ideas of his own; however, whatever was learnt as a child became the beliefs that will influence his inductive reasoning. His idea of such things as relationships, finances, career, to go to college or not, to become an entrepreneur or get a job, etc. would all be influenced by the environment that he was a part of. He would have learnt things that are for his greater good and things that are not.

If we want to change the life we are living, we can; the subconscious mind can be programmed with what the person desires. Some people try to use their willpower to change their results; the change has no permanency because the subconscious mind has no pattern of the new person to build on. As soon as the willpower is removed, things go back to where they were. We see this phenomenon in "yo-yo" diets and "back sliders"; the subconscious mind has no image of the new person. Most people who win millions of dollars in the lottery soon lose it; the subconscious mind does not have a pattern of wealth and does everything to take the person back to where they are comfortable, where their actions are in harmony with their beliefs. The beliefs must be changed for permanent change to take place. If a wealthy person wins the lottery, he or she would not lose it; his or her subconscious mind is accustomed to handling millions of dollars (but then again, wealthy people seldom if ever play the lottery).

It is who we are, our subconscious selves, that determine our life. We are always anxious to change our circumstances, but we do not realize that the change does not happen in our conscious mind; it has to first be made in the subconscious part of our mind. James Allen spoke to this phenomenon when he said: "Men are always anxious to change their circumstances but are unwilling to change themselves." We attract everything to ourselves; the state that we are currently in determines what we attract. If we are climbing a very tall tree in a forest and can only look horizontally; then we will only be able to see and get what is at our level of vision. At 5 feet above the ground; we will get all that is at 5 feet in the forest; we cannot get what is at 20 feet. We have to climb to 20 feet to experience what is there. Our subconscious mind has beliefs that correlate with what is at 5 feet; new beliefs will have to be installed to correlate with what is at 20 feet; Then we will attract THOSE things.

We cannot stop thinking our own thoughts and having various emotions. These, along with the thoughts of others, get into our subconscious mind. We give attention to, criticize and get negative emotions over things that we hear that are not of our concern, not realizing that being sympathetic with these conditions gives rise to emotions that will be expressed in the future. Situations will be created by our own subconscious mind that allows us to experience similar emotions. We are familiar with the term "when it rains, it pours"; everything is magnified and given back to us.

This can be likened to a farmer planting seeds in his garden. The soil does not care what seeds are placed in it, whether the farmer plants seed of corn or the wind deposits seeds of weeds. A kernel of corn will produce a stalk with many ears of corn containing hundreds of kernels of corn; the same thing happens with the weed. The subconscious mind is the garden of pure spirit within us that grows whatever is planted; it is infinitely more fertile than the soil, growth being based on universal laws. Everything is produced abundantly. Persons who are very successful often say that they had not dreamt that they would have had that much success in their lives. People who fail in life will attribute this failure to someone or something, never to themselves. The same laws are at work; we choose the information and the subconscious mind produces it.

It is impossible for the farmer to plant carrot seeds and the soil returns an apple tree. Likewise, it is impossible to imprint thoughts of lack and failure and become prosperous and successful. Each physical seed has an imprint of what it is; likewise, each thought has an imprint of its generic nature. A person who is not successful has in his conscious mind a mental concept of failure. His thoughts follow the same pattern: can't, impossible, someday I will, it's never enough, ingratitude, complaining, I cannot afford, etc.; this pattern is impressed on the subconscious mind and the results are reflected in a life of lack and failure.

We are told to guard the portals of entry into our subconscious mind; the only portal of entry is the conscious mind. Each of us would be extremely upset if someone dumped a pile of garbage in the middle of our living room; we would call the police. However, we are doing much more damage to ourselves when we entertain gossip, complaints and the like; what we give our attention to determines our emotions. Steve Maraboli sums it up as follows: "People tend to be very generous when sharing nonsense, fear and ignorance. And while they seem quite eager to feed you their negativity, please remember that sometimes the diet we need to be on is a spiritual and emotional one. Be cautious with what you feed your mind and soul. Feed yourself with positivity and let that propel you into positive action." Mahatma Gandhi decided that: "I will not let anyone walk through my mind with their dirty feet." He understood that whatever gets in the subconscious mind will become a part of one's life.

The subconscious mind never rests; it is working when the conscious mind is asleep. It is responsible for beating our heart more than 86,400 times each day, three billion times in an average lifetime, for pumping more than 100 gallons of blood per hour, for maintaining the heart and the rest of the body in peak condition; it digests and assimilates our food and eliminates what is not wanted, it makes millions of cells every second and lose pretty much the same amount, it develops the baby inside of the mother, it gets rid of things that don't belong such as viruses and bacteria. It oversees hundreds of thousands of chemical reactions that are taking place in each cell per second, and so much more. It helps the doctor get the patient well; there is the saying that the doctor dresses the wound and God does the healing; the cut on the finger heals itself. The dressing prevents more external harm being done.

The doctor helps us to physically take care of our bodies but only we can take care of our mind. Is that "hole" in the stomach a result of stress, certain bacteria, or eating spicy food? If spicy foods were the cause, entire nations would have stomach ulcers. If it were bacteria, we would all have ulcers. According to William James: "the greatest weapon against stress is our ability to choose one thought over another." That is the answer to all that ails us. The subconscious mind multiplies abundantly all that is impressed upon it; stressful thoughts that are constantly repeated express themselves throughout our body; one such place is the stomach. Choosing positive thoughts that are of an opposite nature work by the same law; they too multiply abundantly and will express themselves, but as something creative, not destructive. Joseph Murphy explains, "As you sow in your subconscious mind, so shall you reap in your body and environment."

Whatever we think, verbalize, and imagine is received by the subconscious mind as an emotion before it can be created. This creation is given back to us in all three areas of our personality: as similar thoughts, ideas, emotions and situations in our physical environment. It is the emotion that has the drawing power to pull to us anything that has the vibrational harmony of that emotion we are expressing.

Our life is a display of the beliefs in our subconscious mind, a reflection of the arrangement of our mind. If we want to experience different circumstances, then we should conceive of ourselves as the person with the different circumstances; everything that we need for this to occur is within each of us. We will then attract those circumstances from the

Infinite that is within us. We have a power within us, and we do not know that it is there. Like the farmer who, not knowing what diamonds looked like, left his farm that contained acres of diamonds to go search for them elsewhere; we leave the power within us to go search for it on the outside of us; from other individuals, from the government, from what we have already unconsciously used the power to accumulate, such as money. We cannot change the inherent nature of the subconscious mind; it will continue to create in abundance whatever we impress upon it. Whatever is created, we experience. That is the life we live.

> *"Even when I was in the orphanage, when I was roaming the street trying to find enough to eat, even then I thought of myself as the greatest actor in the world. I had to feel the exuberance that comes from utter confidence in you. Without it, you go down in defeat."*
> *—Charlie Chaplain*

CHAPTER 5

THOUGHTS: OUR TOOL

> "Thought is a power in itself, one of the great forces of the Universe, and ultimately the greatest of forces, directing all the others."
> —Thomas Troward

Within every human being there is a power hiding in plain sight. We use it every day; in fact, it governs our lives, so we cannot help but to use it. It is the most powerful form of energy: our thoughts. It is the only tool that our Creator gave us with which to construct our lives.

Henry Van Dyke in this poem captures what thoughts are and what they can do:

> "I hold it true that thoughts are things;
> They're endowed with bodies
> and breath and wings;
> And that we send them forth to fill The
> world with good results, or ill.
> That which we call our secret thought
> Speeds forth to earth's remotest
> spot, Leaving its blessings or its woes
> Like tracks behind it as it goes.
> We build our future, thought by thought,
> For good or ill, yet know it not.
> Yet, so the universe was wrought.
> Thought is another name for fate;
> Choose, then, thy destiny and wait,
> For love brings love and hate brings hate."

Our thoughts are the product of our mind, and the only action of the mind is the thinking of thoughts. The thought is the originator of the words we speak and write, the images we have in our mind and the emotions we feel. The emotionalized thought is a spiritual seed, a mental force that has the power and inherent character to express itself.

I impress the thought of what I want on my subconscious mind. Through the powers of Universal Subconscious Mind, the thought that I impressed eventually attracts to itself all that is required to express itself; this expression I experience as my life. How this is done remains a mystery; the Infinite Intelligence that is in us knows the "how". Thoughts of success will eventually bring more success; thoughts of lack will always bring poverty. Our mental state, our mental attitude, determines the life we experience.

There is power behind our words, our thoughts. "For no word of God shall be void of power"; the thoughts that we think today, by the power that is inherent in them, create our tomorrows: tomorrow, the day after tomorrow, five years from now, twenty years from now and so on. When the results of our thoughts show up in our lives, we would have forgotten that we had thought those thoughts. Who knows what thoughts we had thought to bring the results; we are thinking all the time and oftentimes we are not conscious of what we are thinking. We have been told to think whatsoever thoughts are true, noble, just, pure, lovely, and of good report; this becomes our own background murmurings that sets us up for bringing to us the essence of those thoughts.

My thoughts were "I wonder what it would be like to be at home in the evenings for an extended period, not having to go to work". A few months before the 2016 Thanksgiving Holidays, I told my co-workers that I would go ahead and prepare a meal for them because I would not be preparing meals at Thanksgiving or Christmas. Sure enough, both came true; I ruptured my Achilles tendon in October and was away from work for five months. I did not prepare meals for Thanksgiving or Christmas and I experienced the feeling of being at my home in the evenings, not having to go to work. These were not negative thoughts but something that can be perceived as negative happened. Getting paid for five months without working, being chauffeured, meals catered by others, shopping done courtesy of others, getting much needed rest can also be the silver lining in that cloud.

Those thoughts may also not have had anything to do with what happened; the important thing is to find the good in what happens. We at times can look back and associate an event with the direction of our thinking, but not always. The important thing is to rebound from what is perceived as negative, (it is neither positive nor negative. It just is; we color it as positive or negative), consider it a lesson learnt and move on to greater things. All thoughts that we emotionalize, give attention to, contemplate will materialize as situations, experiences or things in our mentality, our spirituality, our body, our pocketbook, our environment. In whatever form they materialize, the person doing the thinking is affected.

We are thinking all the time and unknowingly are planting seeds in a spiritual environment. We are nurturing the ideas that we plant, consciously or unconsciously, by our thoughts. If we plant nurturing seeds of faith, gratitude, a general positive attitude, or destructive seeds of doubt, fear, a general negative attitude, these also will grow. They will grow to respectively support or uproot the original ideas. The attitude we have about the rain, the traffic, our family, the government, the past, the present, the future all impact what we have planted. A positive vibration is a positive vibration whatever the source, and those will help nurture what is planted; a negative vibration is a negative vibration whatever the source, and those will uproot what is planted. Allowing the source of our thoughts to come from our indwelling spiritual self will always grow what we have planted. Allowing the thoughts to come from our current situations, oftentimes lead to the uprooting of our ideas.

In photosynthesis ($6CO_2 + 6H_2O \xrightarrow{\text{☼☼}} C_6H_{12}O_6 + 6O_2$) the plant uses the atoms of carbon, hydrogen and oxygen from water and carbon dioxide along with energy from sunlight to make carbohydrates. We cannot see the CO_2, nor the water as it is taken up by the roots; neither can we see the process; but we see some of the finished products, such as potatoes, tomatoes, and carrots that we consume as food. The other unseen product oxygen goes to impact many other lives that we are not aware of. The spiritual seeds that we plant also change lives that are far removed from ours.

Each thought carries a certain frequency of vibration, and each of these frequencies carry information; its own quality is the fingerprint of that thought. Negative thoughts that result in emotions of shame, sorrow, hate, worry, fear and indifference have vibrational frequencies that are lower than positive thoughts that result in emotions of abundance, joy, gratitude, success, forgiveness, health and enlightenment. The thought frequencies of the Divine Energy in us are the highest that are attainable and our thoughts, our words are channels for the expression of these frequencies. Negative thoughts block and are resistant to the flow of this Divine energy; therefore, what can be carried out when this energy flows through us can never be accomplished; it is blocked by negative vibrations. Our thoughts and our spoken words produce the same results; "There is a strong analogy between a spoken voice and a mental voice. To think is to speak low, to speak is to think aloud." - Neville Goddard.

A fish lives in the sea. It is surrounded by water. Humans live in an environment surrounded by thoughts. In the sea there are animals such as sharks that pose a danger for the smaller fishes; likewise in the pool of thoughts that man inhabits, there are also vibrations that pose a danger; negative, destructive thoughts that have low vibrational frequencies such as hate, prejudice, malice, jealousy, doubt, and fear pose significant danger for humans. One could say that the only danger we face are negative thoughts.

We are all connected. We are all a part of Divine Mind; thought vibrations reproduce themselves and they cannot be destroyed. Every thought that has been thought still exists; it is available for anyone to receive. To receive any thought, one has to be on the vibrational frequency of that thought.

Different thought frequencies stimulate different parts of the brain. If we keep thinking the same types of thoughts, then certain areas of the brain will never be stimulated. If we are always thinking of survival, both as an individual and as humanity overall, the areas of our brain that can receive thoughts of creativity will never be stimulated.

We can only receive the thoughts from where our attention goes – where attention goes, energy flows. Our Creator is sending us 'brand new sparkling high energy' thoughts all the time in response to a need for a change in our situation. However, if our attention is focused on the external world, on survival, on what is wrong, on what is not working, then we can never pick up the vibrations coming from the inside. We create more of what we give our attention to, and so if that attention is directed to what we are living then we continue to create more of the same, and life then becomes a merry-go-round. Shift to thoughts on the life we want to live, and we get off the merry-go-round and find ourselves on an upward path.

If we fix our attention on the opposite of what we do not want, we would be forced to look inwards. Oftentimes what we do want is not yet created; we must create it, and it is only created on the spiritual plane. The Law of Attraction is always at work. Its position is the matchmaker of the universe; it matches vibrations that are like each other. Whatever we keep thinking about emotionally, whatever we keep giving our attention, will sooner or later show up in our lives; the Law of Attraction makes this possible.

We can discern the nature of the thoughts we are entertaining by our feelings because feelings are the conscious awareness of vibration. How are we feeling? That's the frequency that we are transmitting, and at that moment, we attract to ourselves thoughts of a similar frequency. Our feelings at our place of work tonight knowing that we will be jetting off to an all-expenses paid vacation in twelve hours would be very different if cleaning house and doing laundry were what we had to look forward to. The job is the same, but what is anticipated is different; therefore, the thoughts are different. The person who is working a plan for his or her future will have a vastly different thought pattern from the person who has no plans for the future. Some people are happy most of the time, some are sad most of the time; some are anticipating a bright future, and some are expecting a dull future. Their thought vibrations will be different. A child is more excited on Christmas Eve than on the evening of Christmas Day; there is nothing to anticipate as all of the gifts have been opened.

One may not be aware of his or her habitual thoughts; however, the result in the person's life always tells. James Allen at the turn of the twentieth century tells us that our life is our looking glass, the reflection of the thoughts that we have been thinking.

Without understanding, we believe that life threw us a "curb ball." With understanding, we realize that we threw out some 'curb ball' thoughts that resulted in life throwing back at us what those thoughts created: the "curb ball".

How do we get off the merry-go-round we have created for our lives? Our thoughts are based on the ideas we think from, so different ideas are needed to think from. If our ideas are from the same set of ideas, from the same thought pool, then the results will remain the same. This is like a person who changes jobs that provides a few dollars more per hour; learning something different would make a significant change in his or her earning power, to enable the move to another box or another rung up the ladder. The new idea results in a new mental attitude, significantly different from the usual thought pattern. The scriptures do tell us that to have a new mental attitude results in transformation: a significantly different experience. The surest way to transform is to focus on our dreams and to go after them. The goals that we set to go after these dreams empower us to become all that we were meant to be. The desire that we have is the spirit in us seeking expansion and further expression. It will never give us a desire that we cannot fulfill; however, we have to grow to fulfill spirit's demands.

Earle Nightingale spent fifteen years searching for the key to success and the key to failure; he did not buy into the idea that wealthy people were unhappy, which naturally leads to the conclusion that poor people are happy. We all know that this is not so; poverty results in more problems in the world than wealth does. There are wealthy people who are happy, and there are wealthy people who are unhappy. There are poor people who are happy and there are poor people who are unhappy. A person's financial status has nothing to do with whether he or she is happy or sad. What wealth, poverty, success, failure, happiness, unhappiness has to do with, is the state of the person's mind. Earle said that he had found the key to success and the key to failure: the way we think. "We become what we think about." Our subconscious mind is the path to the creation of what we think about.

We all have the same mind, the mind of our creator. Neville Goddard tells us that the rich man, the poor man, the beggar and the thief all have the same mind; the difference is in the arrangement of the mind. Each mind is arranged to attract what is necessary for the person to become what he or she is conscious of, namely: a rich man, poor man, a beggar, or a thief.

The arrangement is determined by the thoughts the person chooses to give attention to; that is what makes the difference. Is the arrangement for wealth or for poverty, for success or failure, happiness or unhappiness? The results tell it all. No one knows of the thoughts except the person who has them; however, everyone sees the results.

> *"You are today where your thoughts have brought you; you will be tomorrow where your thoughts take you."*
> —James Allen

CHAPTER 6

WHAT DO YOU WANT?

"You always know more clearly what you <u>do</u> want when you are faced with what you <u>do not</u> want. But whether you are consciously aware of it or not, all day, every day, you are giving birth to new desires that are being born from the details of the life you are living..."
—Ester and Jerry Hicks

Some people may not know what they want; however, we all know what we do not want. What we want is the opposite of what we do not want. A sickly person wants the opposite; health. Who wants a child that is non-productive? We all want one that is productive. A relationship that is tumultuous is opposite to one that is peaceful. We can come to a decision on what we want when we know what we do not want.

Over a century ago, James Allen told us that man is anxious to change his circumstances but is unwilling to change himself. If we did not know how to do this, the scriptures guide us by telling us to be transformed by the renewing of our mind which Thomas Troward explains as: "The Creative Power is inherent in our Thought." Bob Marley tells us to "Emancipate yourself from mental slavery, none but yourself can free your mind;" and William James, philosopher and psychologist from Harvard, considered to be 'The Father of American psychology', also stated more than twelve decades ago that: "The greatest discovery of my generation is that a human being can alter his life by altering his attitude." Earle Nightingale later defined attitude as the combination of our thoughts, feelings and actions. Different people from different eras have been pointing us in the direction on how to get what we want.

To have more and do more we first have to be more. The laws of the universe dictate that this is so. The Law of Attraction can only bring to us what we are, not what we would like to have. We can bring what we want to ourselves by mere willpower; but as soon as that power is directed at something else, then all that it had brought will be gone. When our spirit acquires a new consciousness, then all that is contained at that level of consciousness, we can attract without much effort. Not by might nor by power, but by my spirit says the Lord. We can be, do or have anything that we have the consciousness of, anything that feels natural to us.

The term 'create' is often used casually; we say a person creates, but only the Creative Intelligence within us has the power to create. Man, chooses what he wants, and the power in the individual creates it. We perform actions to make things happen (this we refer to as creating), not realizing that the universe guides us to those actions to fulfill the thoughts we have chosen.

Let's consider the possible conversation and activities with Jane and her mom in preparing for Jane's birthday party. Jane had told her friends that she was going to have a cake for her birthday.

Jane: Mom, I told my friends that I am going to have the biggest cake ever for my birthday. Can you make me a chocolate cake?

Mom: Sure Jane; I need you to describe the cake to me.

Jane: I want a really big cake, like this big (draws an imaginary circle on the dining room table), and I want a chocolate unicorn with a white head and tail sitting on top of the cake. I want him sitting smack in the middle.

Mom: Is that all?

Jane: And I want white and brown chocolate frosting with big and small swirls. *She ponders for a moment.* And yes, I want the unicorn to be sitting in a field of M and M's - - blue, green, yellow, pink and white.

Mom: Is that it? Are you sure?

Jane: Place a few of the M and M's on the side of the cake, and that's it.
And I need the cake to be round.

She tells Jane to prepare the cake pan, and then to stay out of the kitchen. The cake will be brought to the party room when it is done. Mom goes to the refrigerator and cupboard to see what's available. There is pineapple, eggs, carrots, sugar, butter, flour, chocolate powder, spices, toppers (Unicorn, Donald Duck, Pocahontas), chocolate frosting, a large box of M and M's, pineapple frosting, baking powder and milk. Since Jane wants a chocolate cake her mom chooses the right ingredients. sugar, butter, flour, M and M's, chocolate powder and frosting, eggs, baking powder, spices and milk.

Mom uses the cake mixer to prepare the batter which she then pours into the pan Jane had prepared. It is placed in the oven at the proper temperature and in an hour's time the cake is baked. She decorates it according to the specifications Jane had given her. While the cake is being baked Jane went ahead and prepares her birthday table with balloons, tablecloth, and a place to receive the cake.

She is bouncing with excitement because she smells the cake baking. She is preparing the table for the party and so she does not even think of asking: "is it done yet, when is it going to be ready?" When everything is done Jane and Mom places the cake in the middle of the table, the place Jane had prepared to receive it. Jane's eyes popped when she sees the cake. She is ecstatic; mom had added a few other unicorns to make a family of unicorns and she had added some 'grass' in which the baby unicorns were playing. They were really playing in a grassy field with colored balls.

Let's use this as an analogy to what happens when we ask. Jane is any one of us; she has a desire (in her conscious mind). Did she bake the cake? No, her job was to ask for what she wanted; to form a picture of it in her imagination, which was then transferred with emotion to her mom (her subconscious mind). Her mom knew what needed to be done because the image in Jane's mind was transferred to her mind. Jane had to take some action, she prepared the cake pan to receive the batter and the table to receive the finished product.

Mom then used the limitless contents of the cupboard and refrigerator, as well as the forces at her command - cake mixer, oven and the kitchen - (collectively Universal Subconscious Mind) to fill the order. Notice that Jane was not in the kitchen getting in the way, neither was she asking 'how' and 'when'. She had complete confidence, faith and belief that her mom is making the cake. She smelt the 'fumes' coming from the kitchen, that told her the cake is being baked. When she saw the decorations, she realized that she got more than she had asked for - an entire family of unicorns.

The entire production team, ensemble and props are in each of us. When we give an image over to the Creative Intelligence in us, we will be guided to take some action; this will be miniscule compared to what is necessary to complete the finished product. The finished product was much more than what she had expected. How often have we heard people describing their success say: "not in my wildest dreams did I expect all of this?" Likewise, we hear from those at the other end: "When it rains, it pours."

There are certain questions we can ask ourselves; one such question is "where did the picture in Jane's mind come from?" It must have existed somewhere; how did she put it together? It doesn't matter what we put together in our mind; the ingredients, the different pieces are already created and are somewhere. That somewhere is Universal Mind; the essence of what is 'stored' there comes through to us as a thought that gets transformed into an image in our mind. We manipulate that image based on the concept of ourselves until we get what we want. We hold steadfast to our desire, and the powers and laws operational in the spiritual part of our personality bring all the means operational on the physical plane (people, situations, things) to manifest the image. We just choose from what is housed in the spiritual part of our personality, and that is whatever it is we can think of. We can choose the good, the bad and the ugly; it is all there, all at different vibrational frequencies. However, to receive what we have asked for, we get on its frequency.

When we want to improve who we are as a person, the process is the same. There has to be a deep desire for change. The Creative Intelligence must have an image and the emotions of what it will be like when our desire is fulfilled: the type of people we will be interacting with, the places we will be visiting, the things we will be doing, etc. Our spiritual self will be molded into that new person who will sooner or later be reflected in our personality. We will then start to view the world from this new perspective; our choices will be different; the new person has been created. Prayer is the major element involved, meaning we must believe that we are that person, and we will become that person.

The new person remains so for now, until another desire is born. It has to be so because we are the channels through which the God in us expresses Itself. It is always for expansion and fuller expression; It cannot be more than the perfection that It is, and It is always calling us toward that perfection. Dr. Emile Cady says it like this: "Desire is God tapping at the door of your mind, trying to give you greater good." We then become an expression of the spirit in us.

We choose the ingredients: confidence, poise, tolerance, courage, independence, less weight, more weight, more joy, peace, assertiveness, charisma; the ingredients are endless. Then we put the picture together in our mind of this new person going about his or her daily activities. The spirit, being responsive to suggestion, becomes that person.

What do you want to bring into your life? This Creative Power in you creates it. It is amenable to suggestion, and it is in no way limited by precedent. This is how people have created and done things that were never done or created before. It takes its creative direction from the word you give it. This calls for some measure of faith; if you believe it will do what you desire it to do; then it does it; if you believe it can't, then it won't.

Your subconscious mind is ready to give you what you give to it. Since it acts on the dominant of two opposing ideas, getting rid of opposing unwanted beliefs is the first step. In the physical world, if we want a new living room set, we will first have to get rid of the old one. The same principle applies in the spiritual part of our personality.

New thought patterns will replace old thought patterns. Thoughts of "I can't" are replaced by thoughts of "I can;" impossible is replaced with possible.

<u>Write it down.</u>

We are told: to make the vision clear; write it down. Writing causes focus and organize our thoughts. Businesses operate from plans; our life is our business, so we too need to operate from plans.

Make a list of what you want to bring into your life; examine your list carefully to remove ambiguity. You can list material desires, character traits, situations, etc. Where your finances are concerned, write down the investments, the amount you would like to have in your checking account, your savings account, etc. Where would you like to go on vacation; what places would you like to visit? What would you like your giving to be; what charities would you like to be part of? What awards, certifications, and the like would you like to have? What type of relationships would you like to have with family, co-workers and friends? Examine all aspects of your life and write down what you want; however, never put a person on your list. The person who you are absolutely sure you would like in your life may not be the person to satisfy the desires you have; you are operating only from what is available in your conscious mind. Instead, write down the characteristics of the person you would like to have in your life. Your subconscious mind will always provide you with the best—it knows and sees all. It may be more manageable to make a different list for different areas of your life.

Read your list as often as you can and adjust them as necessary. You may add and subtract from the lists and change your mind about certain things. I always smile when I recall a story by Catherine Ponder in one of her books. It is about a lady who wanted plenty of money for Christmas; however, she was not definite about what she wanted: she only said that she wanted "plenty" for Christmas. Well, she ended up getting a lot of fruit cakes, but no money. The Universe takes you at your word.

A few years ago, I went to New York City to visit family. I wrote down a few weeks before I went that I will visit museums and not pay for my meals. I was in a prayer group, so every day I looked at my list focusing on the New York trip. On a rainy Saturday, my son and I were in a long line waiting to get tickets for the museum. A young man who I did not know stopped by me and said: "Excuse me ma'am, would you like to have two tickets for the museum? I have changed my mind about going." I said "Sure, thank you," and accepted the tickets. Of course, I also received all my meals for the three days without having to pay for any. A small idea that illustrates the point; you yourself may regularly have similar experiences.

M.R. had a different approach; instead of writing down what he wanted, he went to an auto dealership and took a picture of himself beside a truck that he wanted for his business. His faith was so strong, he told the salesperson at the dealership that he will be back by the end of the month to get the vehicle including upgrades, he detailed. The truck was for $75,000 and he did not have a dollar in his bank account towards the truck, but he knew: "Ask, and it shall be given". By the end of that day, within a few hours of him leaving the dealership he received a text from his friend which led to the $75,000. While he was having his photo-op at the dealership, his friend had thought about discussing an investment proposition with him; from this discussion both got what they wanted. The dealership told him it would take at least 6 weeks to do the upgrades; however, within a week the dealership found a truck that already had all the upgrades. Another company had ordered the truck, upgraded it and decided they no longer needed it.

A. E. wrote on a 4 by 4 card three desires: that her two children go through college without it being a cost to her and that she would live in an exclusive area of town. In her business, she would move into a penthouse commercial office space, achieve certain professional destinations within a certain time, paid for without the use of loans. After she had written it down, she forgot about it and went about her daily life, always doing what the situation demanded of her. Years later she found the card; all three desires had materialized.

It is told to us to make the vision plain and to write it down; she did both. The universe dictated her activities, brought her the people and circumstances, and her dreams were fulfilled. After the thoughts leave our conscious mind and get into the subconscious mind, the forces of the universe take over. "Thou shall decree a thing and it shall be established unto thee and light shall shine upon thy way,"

You can receive a kettle just as easily as a castle; the only requirement is that you are at the frequency of vibration to receive it; that is, you live in the feeling of the wish fulfilled, your prayer answered. Take the time to make your list, keep yourself in vibrational alignment with what you want, and watch for the results.

Thirteen percent of us have clearly defined goals and only 3% have it clearly written down; could those be the 3% that control 97% of the wealth? 87% of us do not have clearly defined goals or we have no goals at all. Each such person is like a ship in the middle of a choppy ocean without a captain, a crew or a destination; it will be tossed about and will end up just about anywhere. It likely will be shipwrecked. If we want to move from where we are to a better place, simply acquiring material things won't be enough; there has to be a desire for real change, a focus on the new changed state and clearly defined goals. A goal is a statement of what we intend to accomplish, and when it will be accomplished written as if it has already been accomplished.

"I am so happy and grateful now that.................."

We give gratitude for the goal being done, because as soon as we ask, it is given to us.

A goal gives direction to our lives. The universe works with us continuously towards its accomplishment, if we make our vision clear, and in addition, we keep ourselves harmoniously aligned with the Creative Power that is in us. Who knows what the work will entail, and what the path will be? It will be different for each person because the personalities, goals, state of mind, attitude, receptivity, expectations, emotions, faith and belief will be different. Jesus tells us that he of Himself can do nothing, that it is the Father in Him that does the work. The same applies to us. We give the subconscious mind the pattern of the result and it will guide us in our actions, our behavior, towards that end.

We will have what we want when there is the understanding that there is a creative process that operates within our mind; that our thoughts are creative, our emotions attract the essence of those emotions, what we imagine we become and what we impress on our subconscious mind become our life experience.

> *"When you really want something, and you couple that with an understanding of the nature of your spiritual being, and the laws that govern you; you will keep going, regardless of what's happened. Nothing will stop you."*
>
> —Bob Proctor

CHAPTER 7

ALIGNMENT WITH THE IDEA

"In the moment that a new-and-improved version of life is born out of the life you are living, you have the option of aligning with the new idea or resisting it."
—Ester and Jerry Hicks

There is a power in each of us that creates for us what we give our attention to, what we consciously ask for, what we are unconsciously thinking, what we emotionalize. This power is forever flowing through us, in the form of our thoughts that has the potential to fix all that is out of order in our lives. Our thoughts hinder or allow this energy to flow. Positive thoughts allow it to flow freely and we live a life of wellbeing. Negative thoughts prevent the flow, and we live a life of upheavals and disharmony. When we are in synch with this energy, we are pure positive emotion. We love, appreciate, we feel great, invincible, we have trust, faith, peace, tranquility, ease, we know something with certainty, clarity; we are freedom, love and want the same for others. At any point in a person's life, he or she wants to have the best experience. This happens for the most part when we consciously take control of our lives; when we pay attention to the thoughts, images and feelings we choose to entertain. The subconscious mind is guiding each person into various actions based on the mental attitudes of the individual, and it is the actions that determine our results.

Understanding that we each have the ability to choose, we can decide what it is we are experiencing that we do not want and focus on what is wanted, thereby creating a different thought pattern, a renewing of the mind that will produce different results.

Everything is energy, has a vibrational frequency and carries information. The vibrational frequency of whom we are is constantly being given to our Creator; It creates our lives based on these frequencies. This is how we as spiritual beings are supported while having this physical experience. The creative power in us makes everything out of itself and therefore becomes that thing we asked for; It is limitless in Its creativity. This is what is reflected in our physical world as our circumstances. When we receive something that we really want, we express an emotion such as joy, exuberance, or happiness. This is the vibration which when maintained will draw that thing into our physical experience. Our mental attitude determines the vibrational frequency we are expressing. Consider it like this: the Creator in us created what we asked for; It is being held at the vibrational frequency that we would have when we receive it. The catch is, we have to support the vibrational frequency of the thing we asked for at least 51% of the time. We must attract it to us.

Everything already exists but they are at different vibrational frequencies. Because our feeling is our conscious awareness of the vibrational state that we are in, we can adjust our vibration to be in harmony with what we have asked for.

We want something because it will make us feel better. Happiness, joy, peace, contentment, relief, freedom, and independence are some of the emotions that come to mind; these are the states that we are reaching for. The more we keep ourselves in these states; the easier and quicker will our desires be fulfilled.

The instructions given for our mental attitude when we pray alludes to this: "when ye pray believe you already have it and you will receive it." Robert A Russell recommends that: "All negative states must be converted to positive states before our prayers can be answered."

We are also told to go and take care of the issues that we have with our brother or our neighbor before we come to give praise and thanksgiving; before we pray.

Seeking and seeing the best in others reflects what is in us, and of course whatever a person gives out in thoughts boomerangs back to him or her.

Forgiving others, ourselves or a situation helps to place us in that state of mind to receive the good we asked for. Forgiving is taking care of our vibration; everything rests with us.

"The forgiving state of mind is a magnetic power for attracting good." - Catherine Ponder *The Dynamic Laws of Prosperity*

Whatever things are true, noble, just, pure, lovely, of good report, are the things that should form the foundation of our thought world. Loving ourselves, meaning thinking the best of ourselves and wanting the best, is also what we should do for others.

Recognizing the Creative Spirit within ourselves, being grateful for all that we have received and will be receiving, also get us in the mental state of receiving the good things we asked for. The mental attitude of gratitude draws us closer to the source from which all things come. In *The Science of Getting Rich*, Wallace Wattles says this about gratitude: "There is a Law of Gratitude, and it is absolutely necessary that you should observe the law, if you are to get the results you seek. The Law of Gratitude is the natural principle that action, and reaction are always equal, and in opposite directions."

Expressing gratitude translates into you setting up yourself to get more things to be grateful for.

In his book he further goes on to say: "Many people who order their lives rightly in all other ways are kept in poverty by their lack of gratitude. Having received one gift from God, they cut the wires which connect them with Him by failing to make acknowledgment." We should be thankful for everything; the simplest to the greatest.

"The enlightened give thanks for what most people take for granted…. As you begin to be grateful for what most people take for granted, the vibration of gratitude makes you more receptive to good in your life." - Michael Beckwith

Everything comes from the same Source; we request consciously and unconsciously what we want; however, maintaining the proper mental attitude is a part of the plan. We get so accustomed to doing the same things over and over, we believe that we are the ones orchestrating the actions. There is a bigger part of us that guides us into those actions.

Whatever thoughts are not in harmony with what we want will keep us from getting it. It's all about vibrations; the vibrations must match up. If comparing ourselves with others leaves us feeling less about ourselves, then those thoughts must change. Thinking of oneself from a spiritual standpoint, acknowledging that our inner being is one with the creator and that we are channels for the expression of this power can help give us a very powerful mindset where we do not judge or compare ourselves with others. This mindset also translates to how we interact with others; no one is greater or lesser than. Each of us, by the arrangement of the mind, instructs the spirit in us to manifest this arrangement. The aim is to be happy; all the other attitudes will fall in their right places. For each of us, whatever accomplishes that; according to Nike, "Just Do It." It may be music, movies, exercising; the choices are endless.

We are always talking to ourselves; an activity that we cannot help doing. We are forever having mental emotional conversations with ourselves and with others. These conversations show who we really are; they are always creative, and they do show up in our lives. Awareness of our inner conversations is important. However, it is no easy matter to monitor our thoughts. Our feelings are there to guide us to a better mental state.

Guiding our thoughts to the things that we desire will help us avoid the many pitfalls of negative emotions. A mind occupied with a desired future tends to remain positive. Having the vision of what we want is important. We have been told that without a vision the people perish; this applies to not only nations but individuals. In knowing where we are going, we have a vision to be focused on. If in driving your car, you cannot take your eyes off the dashboard you will be certain to crash. That's what happens in our lives when we are concentrating on the things that are happening now; we tend to focus on the negatives. Likewise, if the eyes cannot be taken from the rear-view mirror, that is a sure sign that there will be an accident. People who are stuck in the past cannot move into the future. We are reminded: "Remember not the former things, neither consider the things of old." The things that we have asked for are present in our spiritual self now and will show up in our physical future, the place where we want them to be. Knowledge that it is already a present fact, although in the invisible spiritual world, will give us confidence that it will happen in our physical world. Doubts will be eliminated and faith, being loyal to the unseen reality, will be the dominant emotion.

The ease with which they show up, how they show up and the length of time they take are controlled by each person. They show up only when the person is aligned with the energy that has been assigned to the desires. If getting a new car evokes a feeling of freedom, joy and independence, then to your subconscious mind, a car is equal to freedom, joy and independence; those are the emotions that will bring the car to you, with ease.

We often hear complaints that someone received something unfairly or that some aren't even trying and are receiving benefits. We hear of teacher's pets, brownie points and other such descriptions for persons who are in vibrational alignment with their wants; but can you guess the vibrational status of the complainers and criticizers?

Ester and Jerry Hicks, in their book *The Astonishing Power of Emotions*, reveal to us that: "No one receives anything unfairly. The Law of Attraction responds fairly, consistently, and powerfully to the vibrations that you are emitting; and if what is happening in your experience does not please you, you have only to identify what you prefer, focus upon it until it is easy for you to focus in that way – and then it will be yours."

Complaining and criticizing result in a decrease, just as easily as gratitude results in an increase. The universe guides everyone to action based on their thoughts; being critical of the actions is criticizing God's Modus Operandi. A person chooses his or her thoughts; the universe answers through means unknown to us. It answers the negative thoughts just as readily as it answers the positive thoughts.

There is a quiet part of us that is diligently and ceaselessly creating what the noisy part instructs it to create. All knowledge lies within this quiet that is not only all-powerful but all-seeing. Through the action of quieting the conscious mind as well as the physical body, we connect with the still small voice that lives in the quiet part of us. It is recommended that we habitually, at least twice daily, take the time to connect with this deep quietness. When we periodically quiet our minds during our day we stop our thoughts, even for a few moments. The energy that creates worlds can flow through us without any resistance, and it makes good anything it touches.

Maintaining alignment with the power that creates worlds', results in the abundant life that was promised to us.

What successes have you had in life? Relive them. The size of the success doesn't matter; the feeling is what matters. How did you feel when you parallel parked for the first time? How did you feel when you scored your first 100% on the test, when you first made an omelet that did not fall apart, when you performed your first surgery? Recapture the feeling. The subconscious mind doesn't know whether the emotion is real or imagined; it doesn't care. According to Neal Donald Walsch,

"Feeling is the language of the soul."

Ester and Jerry Hicks in their book, *Ask and it is Given......The Teachings of Abraham*, suggest going on a rampage of appreciation. For five to ten minutes, write or talk about what you love and appreciate about yourself, something or someone else; it may even be a situation, the day you had. Extend the time as you wish. This practice, especially when we are having negative vibes, can get us in a positive place.

Love is the language of the universe. This is not that intense feeling of deep affection for special people in our lives, but the wanting of wellbeing, of good for others and for ourselves. Henry Drummond in his book *The Greatest Thing in the World* considers love to be composed of nine ingredients: patience, kindness, generosity, humility, courtesy, unselfishness, good temper, guilelessness and sincerity. We do practice some or all these ingredients daily and when we do, we are actually loving ourselves. We are then able to give to others; we cannot give what we do not have. Send mental love to people who may irritate you. See them in your mind's eye and send them love, remember that we are connected.

Because no one can do our thinking for us, we take responsibility for the emotions we entertain and the signals we are transmitting; whatever we give out returns to us as a gift.

> *"Your work is to find relief wherever you are"* and *"Your goal is happiness"*
> —Ester Hicks

CHAPTER 8

AFFIRMATION, AUTOSUGGESTION AND SELF-TALK

"You have the incredible potential to be, do and receive whatever you desire, imagine and truly believe. Unfortunately, however, only a small number of people achieve their full human potential because they fail to recognize and harness the infinite power of the subconscious mind- the divinity within and around them."
—Joseph Murphy

No one can rise higher than his or her beliefs; our beliefs are the thoughts that we keep thinking that become impressed on our subconscious mind and are later expressed as our life experiences. Ideas are conveyed to the subconscious mind by repetition, faith and expectancy; it is amenable to suggestion and it doesn't know the difference between what is real and what is imagined. We can take advantage of these characteristics and install beliefs that we want to see expressed. We install these beliefs by affirming them. Joseph Murphy describes an affirmation as "An assertion that something exists or is true."

To ourselves, we can assert that something exists or is true. This is called autosuggestion; instead of getting suggestions from others, we are giving suggestions to our own subconscious mind. Napoleon Hill in his book *Think and Grow Rich* says this about autosuggestion: "Those who go down in defeat, and end their lives in poverty, misery and distress, do so because of the negative application of the principle of autosuggestion. The cause may be found in the fact that all impulses of thought tend to clothe themselves in their physical equivalent."

The challenge then is to impress new thoughts and ideas onto the subconscious mind. Thoughts that we originate feelingly and knowingly will create for us what we want to experience. Whatever character traits we want to incorporate must be suggested to the subconscious mind. It will accept as true only the ideas that the conscious mind feels to be true. Whatever the conscious mind affirms to be true has to be believed.

If a timid person wants to be courageous, the thoughts of being courageous have to be placed in the subconscious mind. For the idea of courage to take root and grow, the conscious mind also has to believe in the truth of what is being affirmed. The diligent use of the imagination to see oneself and feel oneself as being courageous, while affirming courage, accomplishes this.

The scriptures tell us what to do: "Let the weak man say I am strong." The person at some point will say: "I am courageous." Claiming a condition to be true when the conscious mind knows that it is not true can magnify the unwanted condition. In this case the person may end up feeling even more timid. Nevertheless, if you tell yourself something often enough, you will eventually believe it.

One way to overcome this difficulty is to use a two-step process of affirmation. Belief in what you are saying, and thinking is essential; understanding what you are doing and why you are doing it is also important. Words are not just repeated in parrot-like fashion.

The first step is to state with emotion: "Day by day I am BECOMING more courageous". You are, although there is not yet any physical evidence; becoming courageous, a mental event, also abides by the Law of Growth. Nothing happens overnight; absence of evidence is not evidence of absence. (Although the egg looks the same, a chicken takes twenty-one days before the baby chick is hatched). The same happens to your repeated thoughts; the Law of Growth has the same operation in the physical world as in the spiritual world of thoughts. We are just not accustomed to thinking of our emotionalized thoughts growing into what the thought embodies.

We think in pictures, and as such the idea of becoming courageous will lead to images in your mind of you performing courageous acts, of you being courageous. As time goes by, you will notice that in situations where formerly you were timid, you are now more courageous.

At some point you will move on to the second step where you claim the courage you are seeking. Without realizing it, you will become aware of yourself saying: "I AM courageous," and it will feel true. At this point it will be firmly planted in your subconscious mind and engaging in acts of courage will feel very natural.

The subconscious mind is all-knowing and the epitome of intelligence; it knows what the word 'courage' embodies. Simply repeating the word 'courage' to oneself can also impress the subconscious mind.

Whatever method is chosen, the best time to impress these suggestions is just before drifting off to sleep and on awakening when the body is in a relaxed state. These two times are opportune because the activity of the conscious mind that will remind you that you are timid is suspended. The drowsy state that ensues after consuming a heavy meal is also a good time for slipping a suggestion past the conscious mind into the subconscious mind.

How do you know your subconscious mind has received the idea? Recall that you get a reaction or response from your subconscious mind according to the nature of the thoughts or idea that is imprinted on it. Your daily actions are really the reactions of your subconscious mind to that idea that you gave to it, so your actions are a signal that the idea is accepted.

As you repeat your affirmations, ensure that the thoughts are married with emotions; the subconscious mind is the creative mind and the seat of your emotions; emotions are what stirs the subconscious mind to action.

"The effectiveness of an affirmation is determined largely by you understanding the truth and the meaning behind the words; an affirmation is simply your acknowledgment of a universal truth." Joseph Murphy; *Techniques to Unleash the Power of Your Subconscious Mind*.

"Your spiritual DNA is perfect", Bob Proctor; this is a universal truth. Whatever condition you have decided to change is not serving you; you may have lived with it for a long time, but it is abnormal. Our lives are the embodiment of beliefs we have in our subconscious mind. Some of these beliefs have robbed us of the spiritual perfection; we are experiencing various degrees of this perfection. Whatever you are affirming is not far-fetched; you cannot affirm more than your spiritual perfection. If you can imagine it and believe it to be true, then your creative mind will become it and you will have the experience in your physical world.

Health, harmony, abundance, peace, beauty and love are some of the universal principles of our own being; these should be normal occurrences in each person's life. If they are not currently present, they can be affirmed into being. There is a universal principle of health but none of sickness; sickness is an absence of health. Likewise, discord is an absence of harmony, and poverty is an absence of wealth. Since these conditions are due to the absence of the opposite, you affirm back into your life the presence of what is absent. Affirm health in the presence of sickness and do the same for any condition that you do not want; everything has an opposite.

Understanding who you are and with assurance, realizing that you are not claiming anything over and beyond the ordinary - it may be over and beyond for the people whom you are used to doing life with – allows you to live the life you claim. We are all living the life we claimed. Most of humanity claimed it unconsciously and allowed their attention to just wander anywhere, becoming emotional over just about anything not realizing that they themselves were creating their lives. Regardless of what the current situation is, the ability to ignore all evidence of the present and focus and embody what we want is the way to change our circumstances. This requires commitment, discipline and responsibility; the beauty is it can be done anywhere, as it is mainly mental activity.

Scientists say that it takes twenty-one consecutive days of repetition to develop a habit. Therefore, focus on one or two affirmations for that duration or longer if necessary, and your actions will sooner or later become consistent with what is being affirmed. Imagining that you are what you are affirming is extremely powerful. This adds feeling to the affirmation.

For affirmations to be truly effective, they should be active and convey the desired feeling; they should be declared in the NOW. "I am so happy and grateful NOW that I am _____" Now is more commanding than someday.

'I AM' is more commanding than 'I will be'. To say and to feel that you will be, and you hope to be, tells the subconscious mind that you are not; it creates what you are. I am not sick is much weaker than

I am healthy. Saying and feeling that I am healthy tells the subconscious mind that I am.

The creative process begins to act now. There is no past or future; everything is happening now. All that is being affirmed are different states that are already present. Some people are experiencing them right now, but you aren't. Your affirmations are taking you to where you eventually believe the truth of what you are affirming.

You cannot attract more than you feel 'at home' with; your conscious mind must be able to feel the naturalness of what you are affirming. Affirming "I am a billionaire" when you have never earned or worked with one hundred thousand dollars in a month may be too much for your conscious mind to get a hold of. The money is not going to fall out of the skies; the Divinity in you will point your attention to ideas that can produce that type of money. The state of mind can be expanded progressively to receive ideas to produce a few hundred thousand dollars, then a few millions then the billion dollars. Everything requires growth, even the ideas that are being entertained.

What would you do with the money you are affirming? Do you see it being circulated, invested so as to not diminish to zero? What lifestyle would you be living; would you feel at ease socializing with other billionaires? There must be the consciousness, the feeling of what is being affirmed; otherwise it is simply wishing and hoping.

What do we keep saying to ourselves? These are unconscious autosuggestions. We keep repeating the same thought patterns. We address ourselves 'I', 'I am'; whatever comes behind 'I am" we are claiming. There are certain 'I ams' that bring lack, poverty and sickness. I am broke, I am feeling sick, I cannot afford, I have not, I cannot, I am worried, I am nowhere close, etc. Every feeling makes a subconscious impression.

At the back of our mind should always be the question "Do I want to experience what I am thinking and feeling?" It takes time to change what has been instilled the past ten, twenty, forty, fifty, sixty years and beyond; however, the Creative Intelligence in us can accomplish any task we give to it.

Whatever exists in the realm of the Universal must manifest in the realm of the physical; this is law. The affirmations below are to get a new thought pattern in the realm of the Universal, but it begins with our conscious mind.

Every day in every way I am getting better and better.

I am now getting better at everything I do.

I am now successful in all my undertakings.

"As the years go by, I am getting more youthful and useful." - Rev Ike

I am now a magnet for all that is good, beautiful and loving.

My health improves daily.

I am healthy.

I am the best; I expect the best and I receive the best.

"I am so happy and grateful now that money comes to me in increasing amounts from multiple sources on a continuous basis." Bob Proctor

"Vast improvements come quickly in every phase of my life now. Every day in every way, things are getting better and better for me now." Catherine Ponder, *The Dynamic Laws of Prosperity*

I am so happy and grateful now that all my financial obligations are completely paid; quickly, easily and in a Divine manner.

"The Lord is my shepherd; I shall not want." Psalm 23:1

"I love the highest and best in all people and I now draw the highest and best [customers, clients] to me now." Catherine Ponder, *The Prospering Power of Prayer*

'Things are always working out for me now." (Ask yourself: What specific things do I want to work out for me) Ester Hicks

"The God in me knows what to do, how to do it, and does it." Rev. Ike

"Of myself I cannot do it, but the Christ within me can, and is performing miracles in my mind, body and affairs here and now." Catherine Ponder

"I now let go of worn out things, worn out conditions and worn out relationships. Divine order is now established and maintained in me and in my world now." Catherine Ponder, *The Dynamic Laws of Prosperity*

"Lord, I do give thee thanks for the abundance that is mine."

The scriptures have so many passages that can place us in a better place, but they need to be repeated often enough so that our subconscious mind feels the truth of what we are affirming. The creative power in us will create that person that we affirm. We will then attract to us all that is in harmony with this person that we have become.

Contemplate words that can leave anyone in a better place: SUCCESS, BEAUTY, LOVE, LIFE, HARMONY, PROSPERITY, WISDOM, JOY, HAPPINESS, etc. The essence of these is what anyone would like to bring into his or her world. When your subconscious mind gets it, you will be propelled to action to manifest what the word embodies.

Genevieve Behrend in her book *Your Invisible Power* has this to say about words: "In every word you use, there is a power germ which expands and projects itself in the direction your word indicates, and ultimately develops into physical expression."

Repeating the words over and over "Makes the word in all of its limitless meaning yours, because words are the embodiment of thoughts, and thought is creative; neither good nor bad, simply creative."

Write your affirmations on cards and keep them everywhere you can see them or get to them when needed; in the car, pockets, purses, backpacks, in the various rooms of the house, on walls, on the bottom of your computer monitor, on your refrigerator, your bathroom mirror, etc. You are ensuring that you are reminded of them, you will keep thinking about them; they will eventually become a habit. You are creating a mental attitude that rejects the negative thought stream.

A number of affirmations can be recorded and listened to, especially when your mind is in a receptive mode such as when you are drifting off to sleep, or when you are engaged in activities that do not require much concentration such as walking and doing house work. They can become your background audio.

To change our circumstances, we must transform our mind: the subconscious mind.

> *"The form taken by our outward conditions, whether of body or circumstance, depends on the form taken by our thoughts and feelings, and our thoughts and feelings will take form from that source from which we allow them to receive suggestion. If we allow them to accept their fundamental suggestions from the relative and limited, they will assume a corresponding form and transmit them to our external environment, thus repeating the old order of limitation in a ceaselessly recurring round."*
> —Thomas Troward

'Your Secret Operator' is no longer a secret.
—*The Author*

MEET THE AUTHOR

For more than 25 years, Dr. Sonya Hylton has worked in the healthcare industry as a Registered Nurse and Pharmacist. She is the Founder of Life Potential Global and a Personal Growth/Transformational Coach, in collaboration with the Proctor Gallagher Institute.

Dr. Hylton was inspired to help others reach their full potential after becoming involved in network marketing. "I decided after listening to insights given by extremely successful distributors that I would take the time to understand what they understood about achieving one's full potential," she said. "I was further inspired and coached by Bob Proctor who has studied this information for 55 years, and who is widely recognized as the leading authority in the personal and professional development industry."

In her role at Life Potential Global and with the Proctor Gallagher Institute, Dr. Hylton helps clients live their lives to the fullest. "I guide clients through a logical system that unlocks their potential allowing them to achieve their goals and transform their lives," she said.

Finding her new career to be very rewarding, she is enjoying having a "ring-side seat to my clients' incrementally overcoming fear of the future, understanding their past results, achieving their goals; and most importantly, being empowered with this information where they can themselves transfer this knowledge and effect generational changes."

A former high school teacher who continues to work with students, one of Dr. Hylton's goals is to create success programs for schools that focus "on the individual's inner power and the Laws of the Universe."

Learn more about Dr. Hylton's work at www.lifepotentialglobal.com

www.ingramcontent.com/pod-product-compliance
Lightning Source LLC
LaVergne TN
LVHW051504070426
835507LV00022B/2921